WORTH THE WAIT

written and illustrated by Andrée Linnell

First comes love,

Then comes marriage.

Then comes a baby,

In a baby carriage.

But sometimes, it doesn't always work that way.

Sometimes, it's not always that easy.

My journey to you was much, much longer.

My journey to you wasn't breezy.

I had to wait for you longer than most mothers.

I had to pray for you harder than most mothers.

One day, a baby angel came to visit me.

The baby angel brought me so much joy.

But the baby angel couldn't stay.

Why baby angel had to go, we will never know.

The baby angel gifted me a token of hope inside of my heart.

I held onto it while praying for you.

I didn't know your name.

I didn't know if you'd be a boy or a girl.

I didn't know if you would ever come.

But I held onto it, and I prayed for you.

Until finally,

One day,

I saw your heartbeat on a tiny screen.

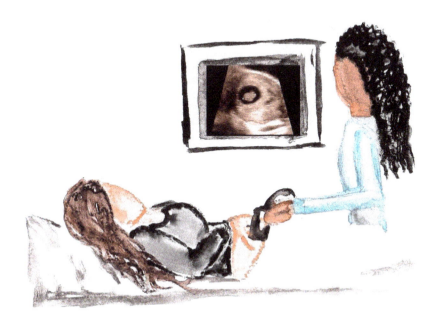

I felt you growing bigger and bigger inside of my belly.

I felt your kicks.

I could even feel your hiccups!

I had fun eating cereal off your head.

I could barely leave my bed!

Growing you inside of me was as special as can be.

Then, one beautiful day, we finally met you.

We finally held you.

We finally named you.

Oh, our sweet rainbow baby, you were worth the wait.

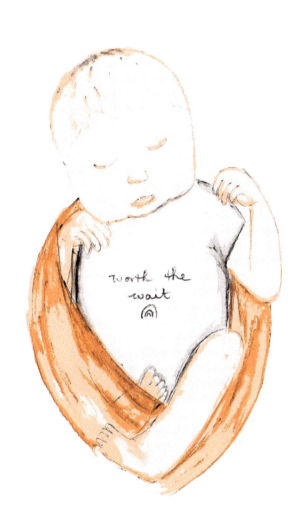

Dedication:

To Coralie, my rainbow baby.

May you always know how much I wanted you

and how deeply I love you.

Mama

Worth the Wait was inspired by my difficult journey toward a healthy baby. I suffered two miscarriages before being blessed with Coralie.

I hope that all children grow up knowing that sometimes, life isn't always as simple as a nursery rhyme. Sometimes, life will throw challenges that you weren't prepared to handle. But, with a little faith and a lot of grit, you can get through anything.

To all the mothers who have experienced this loss: we may have to walk through a thunderstorm before being blessed with our rainbow, but in the end, it is worth the wait.

FriesenPress

Suite 300 - 990 Fort St
Victoria, BC, V8V 3K2
Canada

www.friesenpress.com

Copyright © 2021 by Andrée Linnell

First Edition — 2021

All rights reserved.

No part of this publication may be reproduced in any form, or by any means, electronic or mechanical, including photocopying, recording, or any information browsing, storage, or retrieval system, without permission in writing from FriesenPress.

ISBN
978-1-03-911309-1 (Hardcover)
978-1-03-911308-4 (Paperback)
978-1-03-911310-7 (eBook)

1. JUVENILE NONFICTION, FAMILY, NEW BABY

Distributed to the trade by The Ingram Book Company

CPSIA information can be obtained
at www.ICGtesting.com
Printed in the USA
BVHW020446261021
619827BV00002B/9